Customs of the Arabian Gulf

Arab school children portray their daily life and holiday customs

by Bahia Fakhro and Ann Walko

Illustrations by the students of Kortoba, Kornata and Khuds Primary Schools, Muharraq, Bahrain and Tolaytila School, Dubai, United Arab Emirates.

© 1978 Bahia Fakhro and Ann Walko
All rights reserved. For information write to:
Arab Customs, Box 6023, Hamden, Connecticut 06517, USA, or Bahia Fakhro, Box 1699, Dubai, United Arab Emirates

Designed and produced by Design for Print Ltd, Saffron Walden and London
Printed in Singapore

Bahia Juma Fakhro is a Bahraini Arab living in Dubai, United Arab Emirates, with her husband and three daughters. Mrs Fakhro graduated from Beirut University College in 1964 with a BA in Child Development. She taught psychology, sociology and methods of teaching at the Manama Secondary School for Girls in Bahrain for five years. She also served as Deputy Headmistress of the school.

In 1969 she moved with her husband to Abu Dhabi, UAE, where she was Principal of the Um Ammar Secondary School.

Mrs Fakhro comes naturally by her knowledge of, and interest in, the Arab customs of her area. Her family and her husband's settled in Bahrain two centuries ago. Since that time, as prominent landowners, traders and government officials, they have played a leading part in developing the business and cultural life of Bahrain.

Ann Walko served as Administrative Secretary to the Headmaster of The Jumairah American School, Dubai, UAE from 1975 to 1978. Prior to coming to Dubai Mrs Walko had a varied career as a newspaper reporter, editor, teacher of high school English in the United States and at the American Girls College, Istanbul, Turkey. She moved to the Middle East with her husband in 1975 when his company assigned him to Dubai.

Together with Mrs Fakhro she conceived the idea of using Arab school children's views of their society to educate Western children about life in the Arabian Gulf.

We are especially grateful to Rashed Al Oraifi and Rashed Fakhro, our advisors on cultural traditions, to Jehane Islam and her students at The Jumairah American School, Dubai, who acted as critics of the text, to Diane Charles and to Nancy Cameron for her advice on vocabulary.

For the gathering of these pictures illustrating Arab customs and traditions we are indebted to:
Fatima Hijazi, *Headmistress*, Fatima Sanad, *art teacher*, *Khuds Primary School*; Fatima Abdul Aziz, *Headmistress*, *Kortoba Primary School*; Amina Khunji, *Headmistress*, Shaikha Abdulla Jamal, *art teacher; Kornata Primary School, Muharraq, Bahrain*; Mariam Oumar, *Headmistress*, Leyla Gamil, *art teacher, Tolaytila School, Dubai*; Naima Al Mahmeed.

For: Ian, Nermeen, Mai and Dina

Foreword

اللّي ما يعرفك ما يثمنك

He who does not know you
Does not know your worth

        Arab Proverb

The pictures in this book were drawn by school children living in the Arabian Gulf. These children are part of the community of Arabs who live on the eastern shores of the Arabian Peninsula.

    Since the discovery of oil in the late 1930's in Saudi Arabia, and in the Gulf itself between the late 30's and early 60's, the Arab people have begun to change their style of living. Yet old customs and traditions persist — especially in the celebrations of festivals connected with religion.

    There still remains some of the rhythm of a less hurried, less mechanized way of life. There remains, too, among the Arabs of Arabia an air of courtesy and a generous hospitality in their dealings with the foreigners that are now flooding in to share in their economic development.

    In this book you will see through the eyes of Arab children some of the customs and traditions still important in Arabia. In this way, we hope you will come to know your Arab friends and to 'know their worth'.

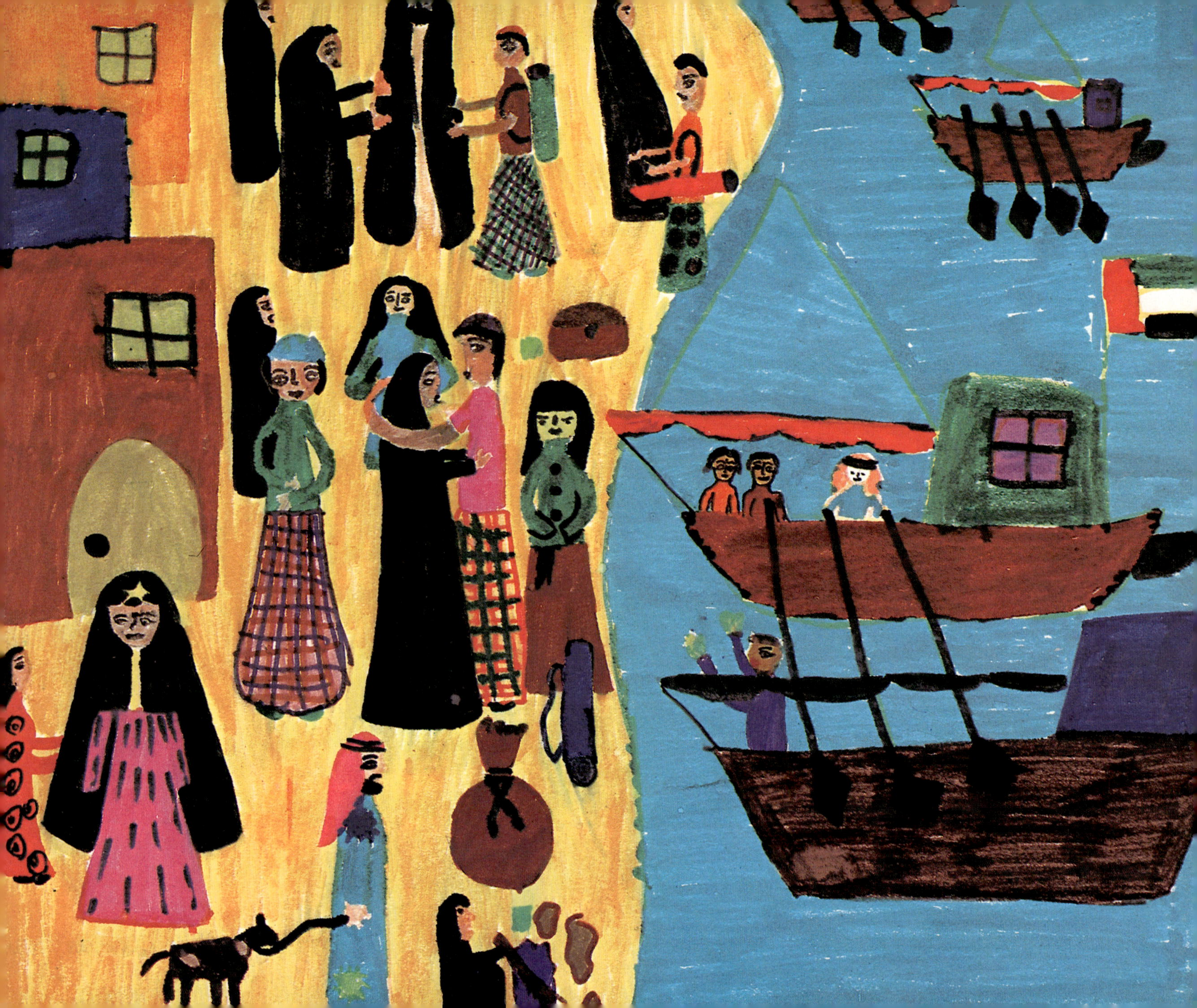

Contents

	Page
Foreword	5
Dishdashas and Darra'as: *Traditional Dress*	9
Al Souk: *The Marketplace*	11
Bagghal: *Vegetable Man*	13
Souk Al Khamis: *Thursday Market*	15
Al Kaaba: *The House of God*	17
Al Masjid: *The Mosque*	19
Al Khatma: *Koran School Ceremony*	21
Al Ghous: *Pearl Diving*	23
Said Al Sammak: *Fishing*	25
Mattar: *Rain*	27
Al Oud: *Incense*	29
Henna: *Wedding Makeup*	31
Al Zawaj: *The Wedding*	33
Al Rizeef: *Men's Dance*	35
Al Muradaa: *Women's Dance*	35
Eid Mubarak: *Holiday Greetings*	37
Salaam El Eid: *Courtesy Calls*	39
Eid Al Adha: *Celebration of Sacrifice*	41
Hiya Biya: *Children's Sacrifice*	43
Al Tubool: *The Band*	45
Al Furaisa: *The Wooden Horse*	47
Girgaoun: *Mid-Ramadan Songs of Praise*	48

8

Dishdashas and Darra'as: *Traditional Dress*

In Arabia the women wear long dresses called darra'as, or kandura. Often these are embroidered with gold or silver thread around the neck, the sleeves and hem. When women appear in public they always wear a black cloak (aba) draped over the head which covers them to the ground. Most women in Arabia wear veils in public, some face masks; they also wear them at home in the presence of men visitors.

If an Arab woman goes to a party or makes an Eid visit, she wears a long, flowing dress called a thob al nashel. This is made of thin colored silk or voil elaborately embroidered in gold or silver.

Young girls do not use veils or masks but cover their heads with a black scarf edged with gold thread. It is called a bukhnag.

Arab men dress in long robes called dishdashas made of cotton in summer and of wool in winter. They protect their heads against the hot sun with a large white or red checked kerchief, a ghetra. It is kept firmly in place by winding a thick black rope, agal, around the head. For formal occasions Arab men wear lightweight brown or black cloaks (bisht) over their dishdashas. These are edged with gold braid.

Men and women in Arabia wear loose, flowing clothes to keep cool in hot weather

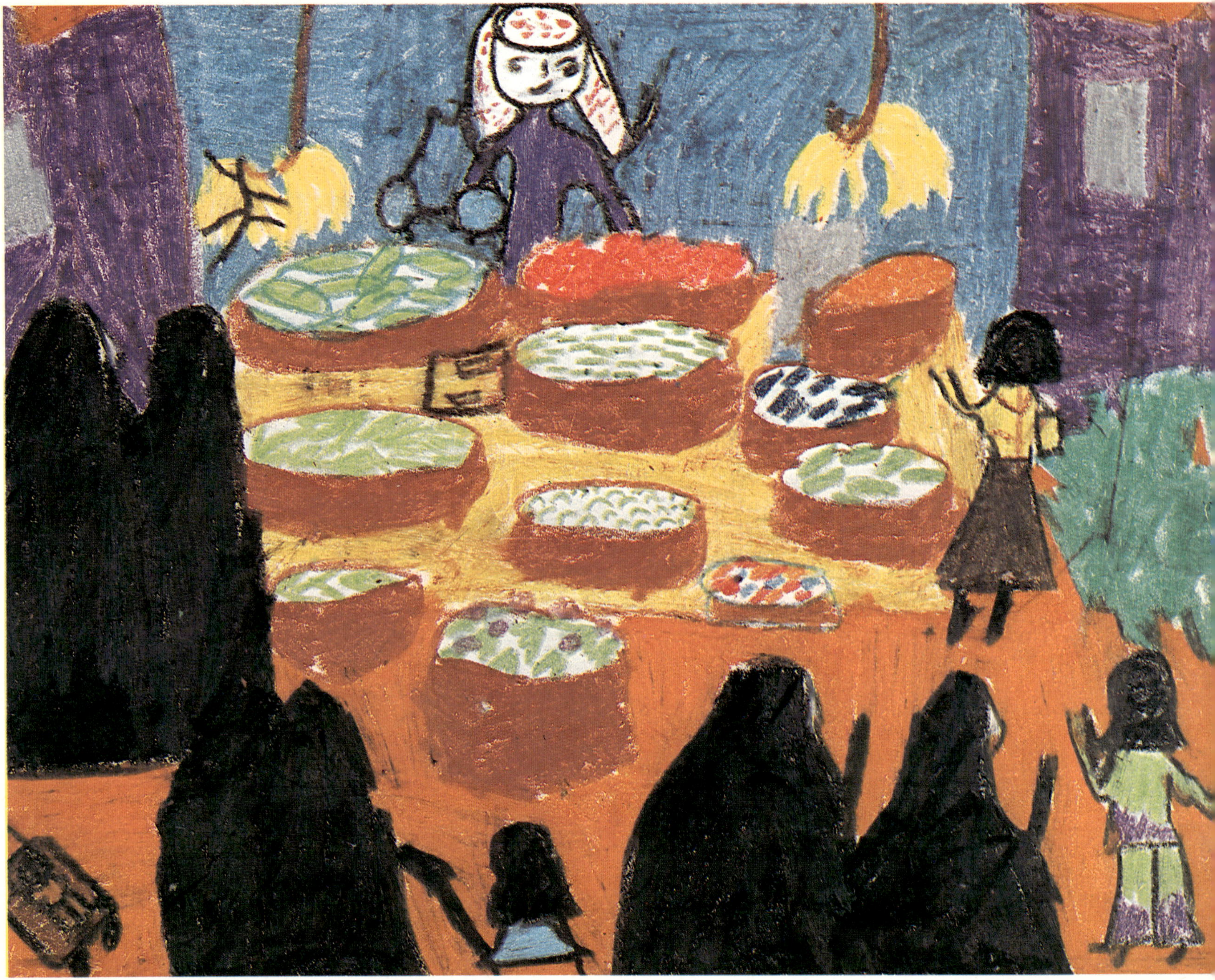

Al Souk: *The Market Place*

It is a small world of many colors, odors, hustle and bustle. A variety of goods are displayed openly for everyone to see, touch and taste. Some shopkeepers sit silently on a stool behind their goods while others call people in for a look in the hope that they'll come and buy. The souk is also a place where the men meet to rest and talk over a cup of bitter coffee.

Souk means marketplace where local people go to buy their food, clothes and other needs.

Bagghal: *Vegetable Man*

Every day of the week Bagghal drives his cart full of vegetables and fruit through the narrow alleys. He shouts loudly so the housewives inside their high-walled courtyards know he is coming. 'Ya aloumi, ya aloumi! Hamid helou, ya aloumi.' 'Lemons, lemons. Sweet and sour lemons.' Sometimes he sings, 'Apples, apples, rosy as a young girl's cheek.' If the women want to buy, they half-open their doors and call to Bagghal to stop. They never buy without bargaining.

Donkey carts are still used to sell food and other goods in narrow alleys which run like a maze across the old parts of the cities and towns.

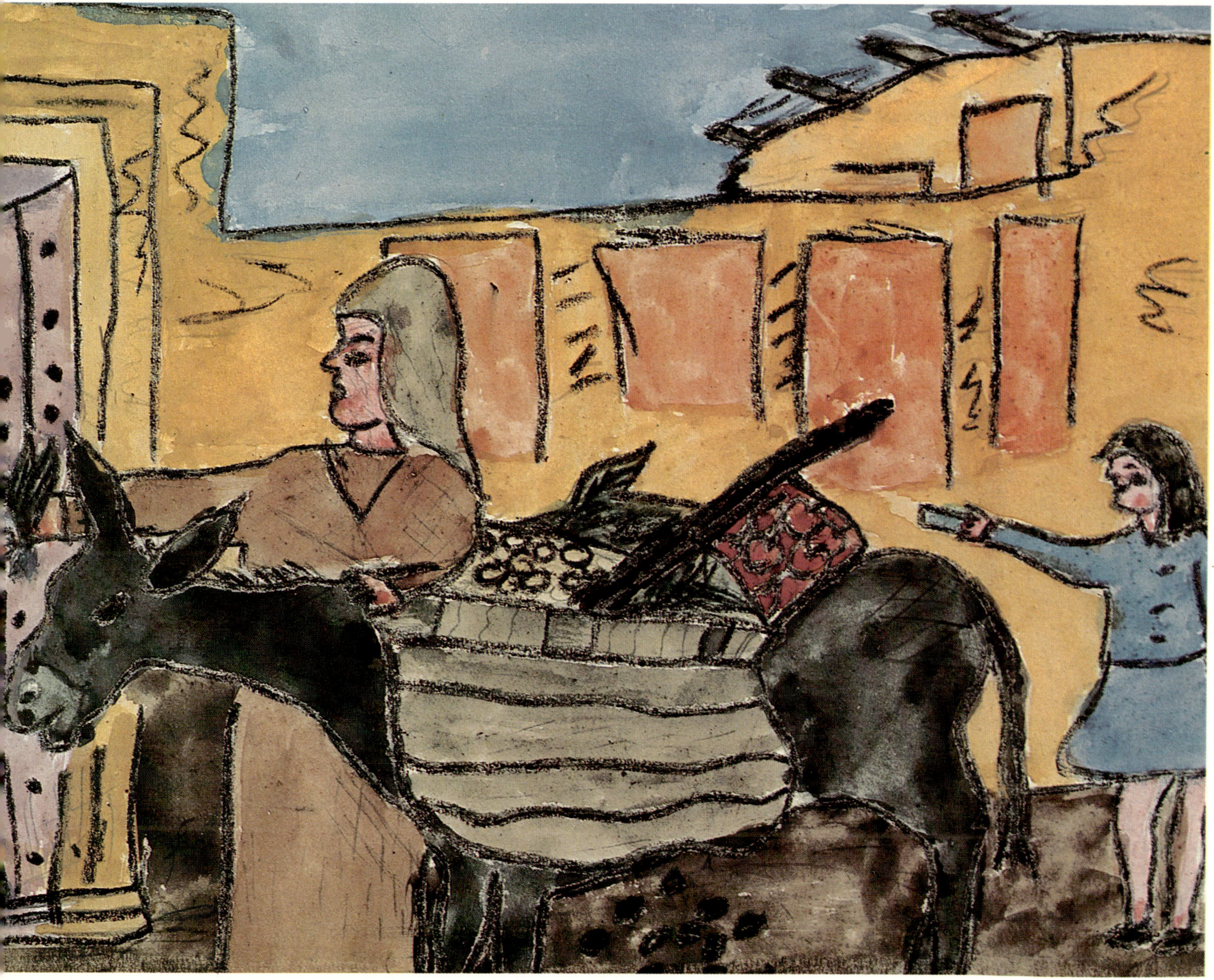

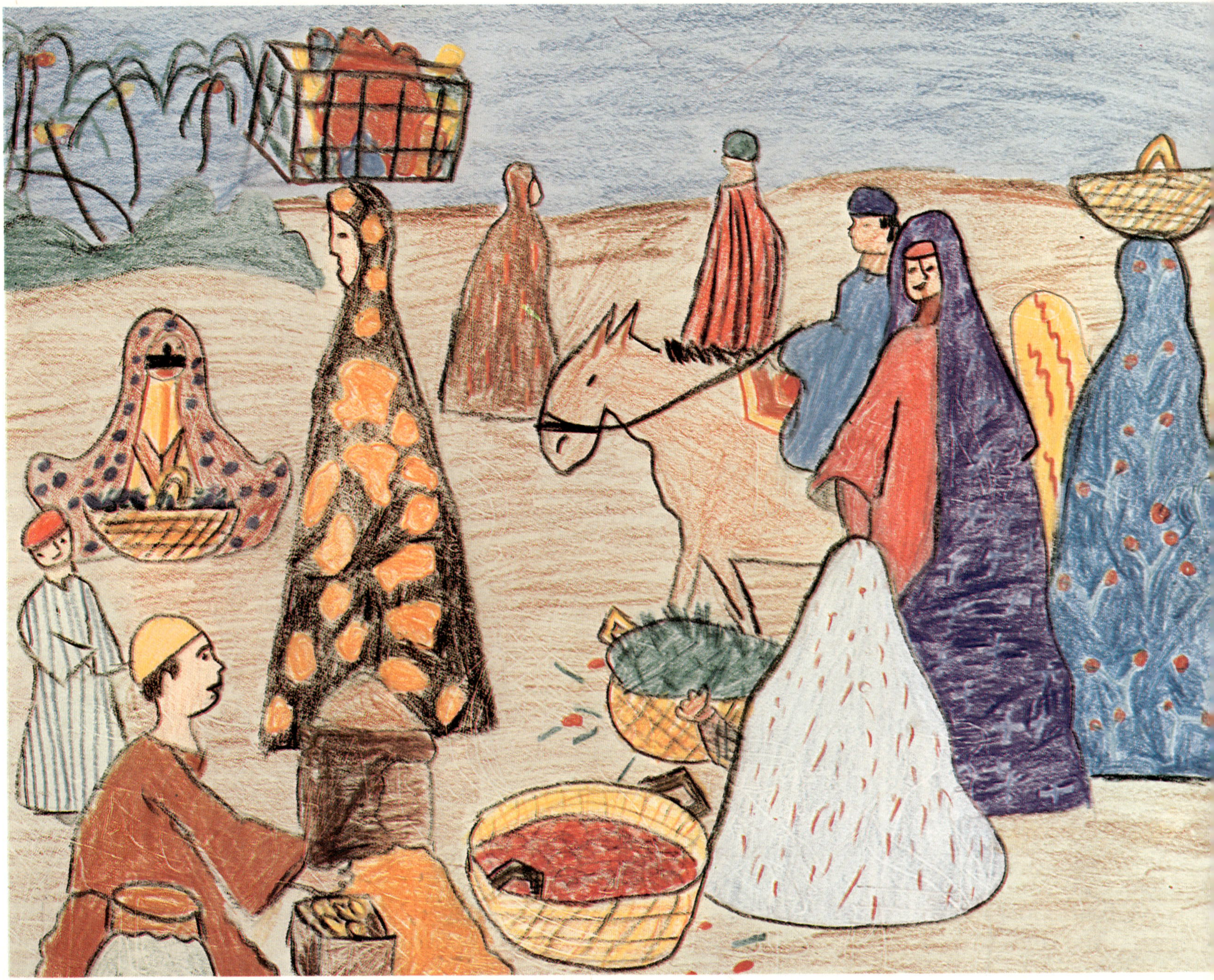

Souk Al Khamis: *Thursday Market*

When we think of Arabia we think of deserts. However, some parts receive enough rain so that food can be grown. Along the north and east coasts where mountains attract the rain clouds water collects deep in the ground. The people living in these regions drive shafts into the mountainsides. They dig tunnels called falaj and pipe the water through them down to the flat coastal plains. With water from the falaj Arab farmers can raise not only dates, but vegetables and some fruits. They till small, irrigated fields where they grow cucumbers, tomatoes, onions, lettuce and melons.

Most days of the week they work hard in the fields. But it is a long-standing custom to hold a bazaar once a week in the center of the nearest village.

Once a week farmers bring their produce into the village square to sell or trade. Men and women set up shop, usually in the shade of a tree.

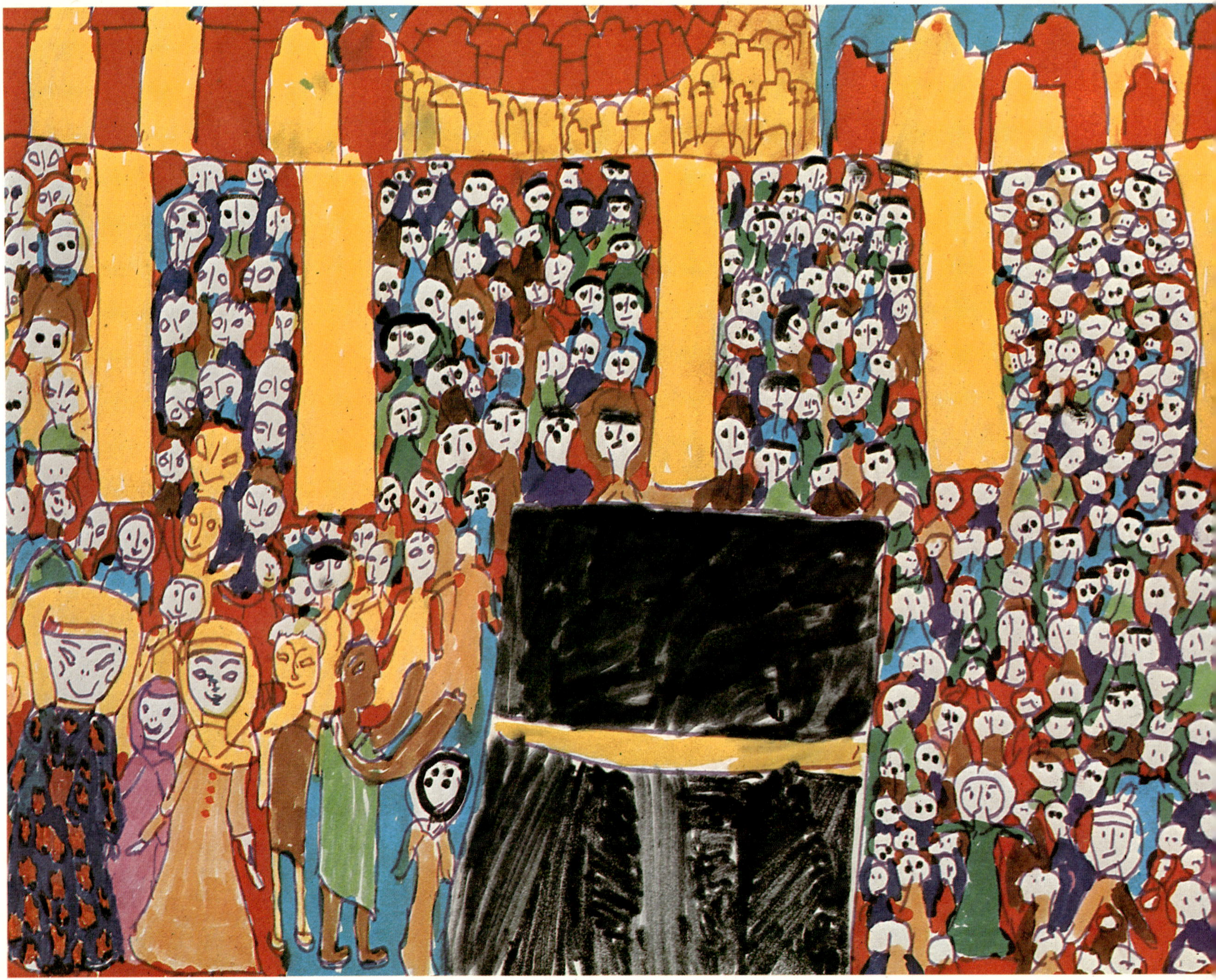

Al Kaaba: *The House of God*

Muslims call it the House of God — not because He lived there — but because they believe His mercy descended on it and gave it meaning.

It is a simple cube-shaped building with a flat roof containing a sacred Black Stone. The stone is set in a silver ring in the south wall.

The Koran says that the Kaaba was built by Ibrahim and his son, Ismail, to house the stone which was given to them by the Angel Gabriel.

Every year more than one million Muslims make a Hajj (pilgrimage) to Mecca to visit this holy shrine. The pilgrims run or walk seven times around the Kaaba chanting their prayers to God. Then they kiss the Black Stone.

According to the Koran it is one of the five duties of a good Muslim to make the pilgrimage to Mecca at least once during his lifetime. The other four are declaring faith in one God, prayer, almsgiving and fasting. After a Muslim has made the pilgrimage he is entitled to be called Hajji, a title of respect.

This most sacred shrine of the Islamic Faith is located in Mecca, Saudi Arabia.

Al Masjid: *The Mosque*

In the mosque the Holy Man (Imam) leads the assembled faithful in prayer. On Fridays at noon he holds a special service in which he reads from the Koran and preaches a sermon.

In the past the Khalifa, the ruler, who was called The Prince of the Faithful also preached. He urged his people to do their duty as good citizens in order to assure themselves a place in heaven.

At prayer time, wherever he is, a Muslim kneels, faces toward Mecca and says his prayers. Mecca, Saudi Arabia, is considered the center of the Islamic Faith. There in AD 630 Mohammed The Prophet proclaimed One God.

The mosque is the holy place for Muslims. From the top of its minaret the Muezzin calls them to prayer five times a day: dawn, noon, afternoon, dusk and suppertime.

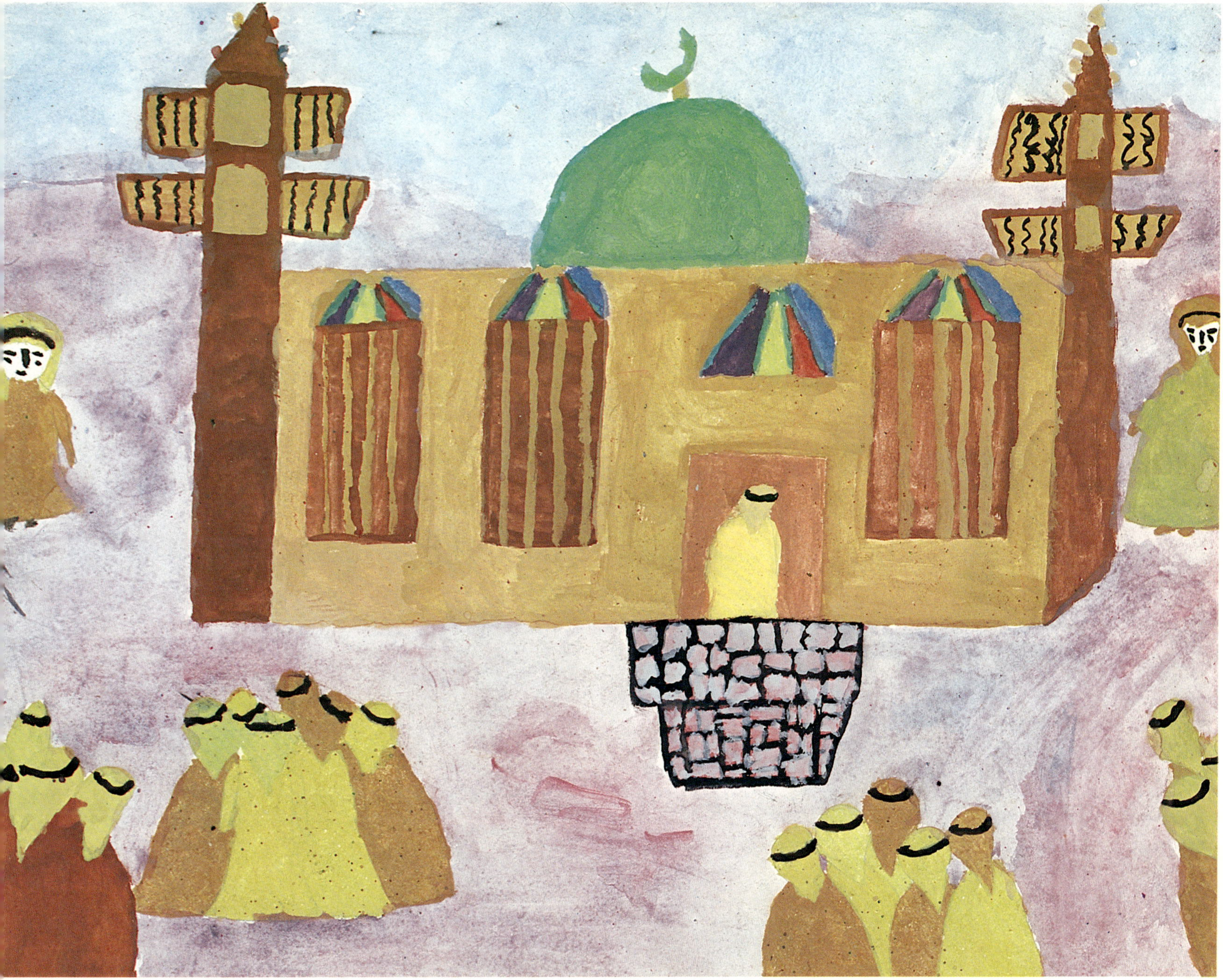

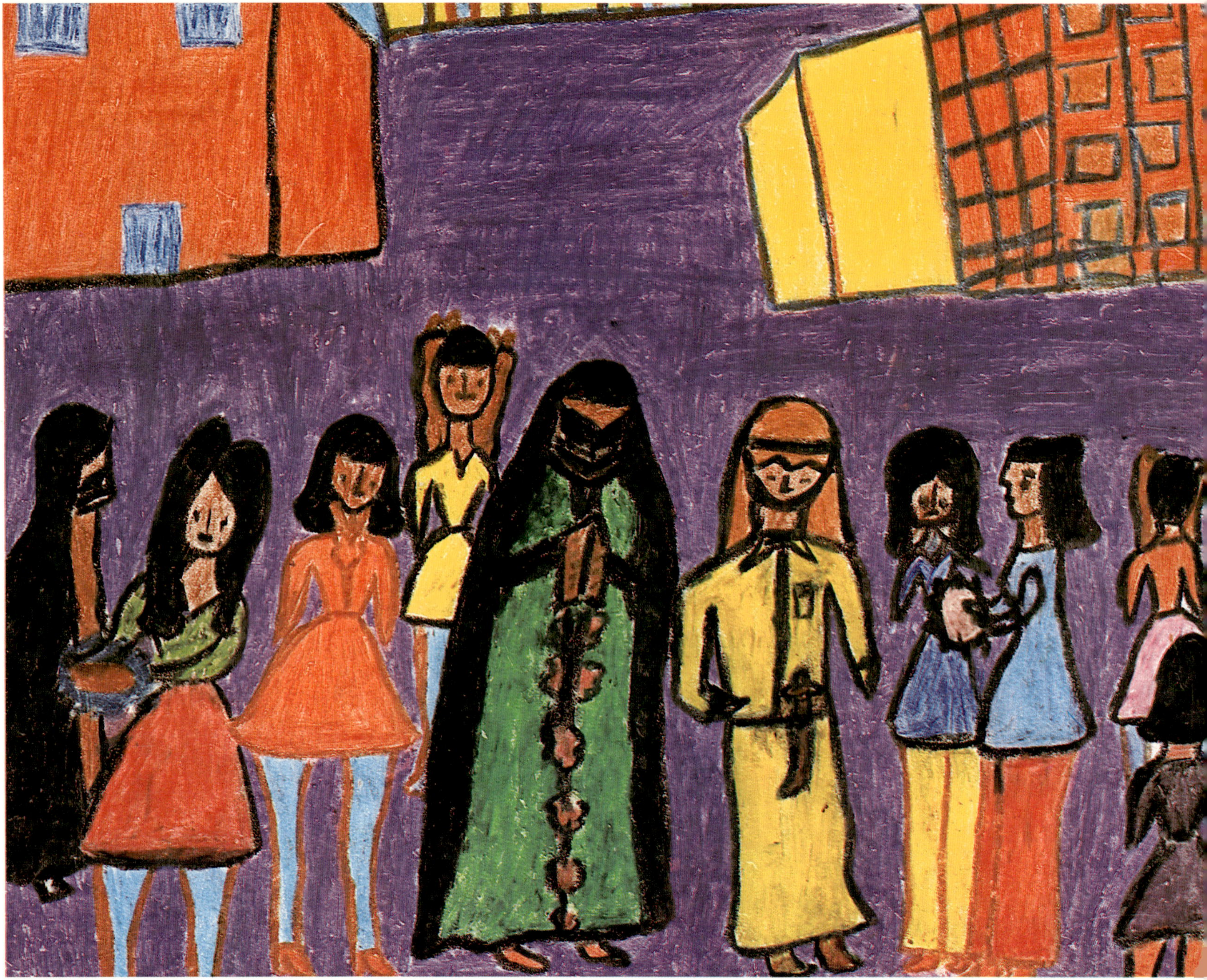

Al Khatma: *Koran School Ceremony*

Before there were any public schools, Arab boys and girls attended private religious schools. There they were taught to read the Koran by a teacher, Al Mutawa. (The Koran is the Holy Book of Islam as the Bible is the Holy Book of Christianity).

Today most Arab children go to public schools. Some also still attend private schools to study the Koran. After Al Mutawa decides a student is able to read the Holy Book well enough, from beginning to end, the parents are notified. They then arrange the Khatma Ceremony. The student dresses in his or her best clothes and is taken by Al Mutawa and classmates to visit friends and relatives. At each home he or she reads brief passages from the Koran. Then those visited give Al Mutawa small gifts of money in recognition of the good job of teaching done.

Al Khatama is the Arabic name for the ceremony that is observed when a child has completed the reading of the Koran.

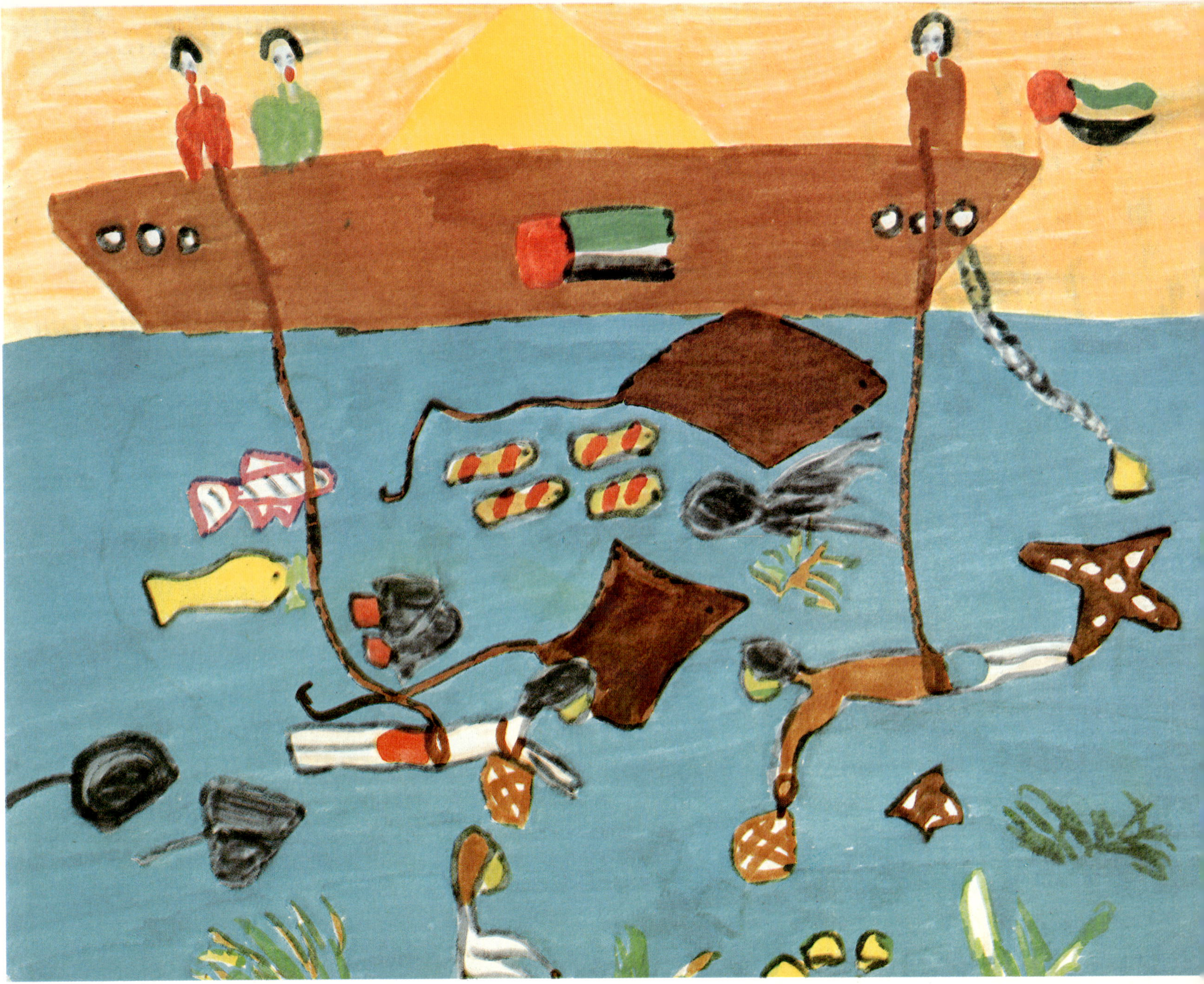

Al Ghous: *Pearl Diving*

For thousands of years, until the discovery of oil, the most beautiful pearls in the world were harvested from the Arabian Gulf. Pearl diving was the main occupation of the peoples living along its shores.

The life of the divers was a very hard and dangerous one. They had to be careful as they worked to avoid sea snakes, giant sting rays, and sharks. They were armed only with the knife used to pry the oyster shells from the beds.

A diver hung a basket around his neck, pinched his nose with a wooden peg to keep out the water and jumped overboard. When he jumped he had two ropes tied around his waist. One rope had a rock tied to it to help him sink to the bottom. The other was used by his helper on deck to pull him up when he signalled that his oyster basket was full. A very important crew member was Al Nahan, the singer. After a day's diving, as the men rested, he sang songs about their homes and loved ones.

In the shallow waters of the Arabian Gulf there are large oyster beds. At one time hundreds of ships anchored over these beds while divers collected the oyster shells and pried them open, looking for pearls.

The memory of leaving you has
  left me sad and weak
I shut my eyes to forget you
But my troubled heart won't let me
If your heart, my pretty one, is
  broken like mine
Why do you not treat my weeping
  wounds
Before the body grows old and
  withers away
One time you invite me, and another
  you let me go
But if you are fair, you will love
  me . . .

Today a few men still dive for pearls but most prefer to work ashore where the pay is higher and the jobs are less dangerous.

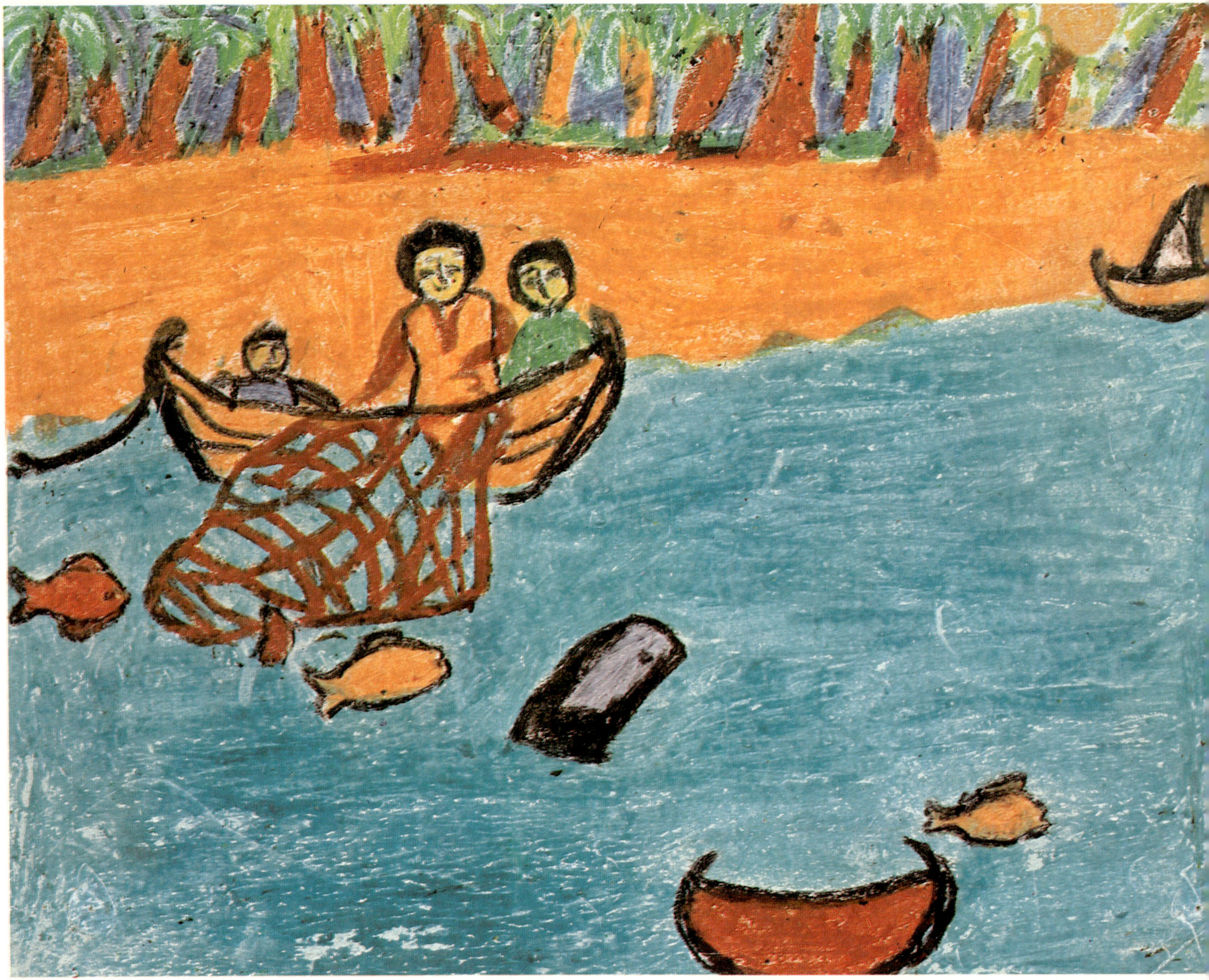

Said Al Sammak: *Fishing*

Since the discovery of oil and the development of cultured pearls by the Japanese, the pearling industry has almost disappeared. But fishing has continued because fish is the favorite food of Gulf Arabs. Fishermen sail in small boats far out in the Gulf where fish are plentiful among the coral beds. In shallow waters they build traps (Hadra) to catch fish which look for food and shelter near the shore. Many also use steel wire nets (Shabak) close to the beach.

In the old days Arabs living on the edge of the Gulf earned their living by diving for pearls and by fishing.

Mattar: *Rain*

When rain falls it is an exciting time. Town children dance and splash in the puddles. One of the songs they sing:

God send us more rain
And have mercy on us,
Your slaves
Rain, beat down
On our new house
Its iron drainpipes
Are strong
Come down rain, come down

It rains very little in the Arabian Gulf; perhaps three to four inches each year.

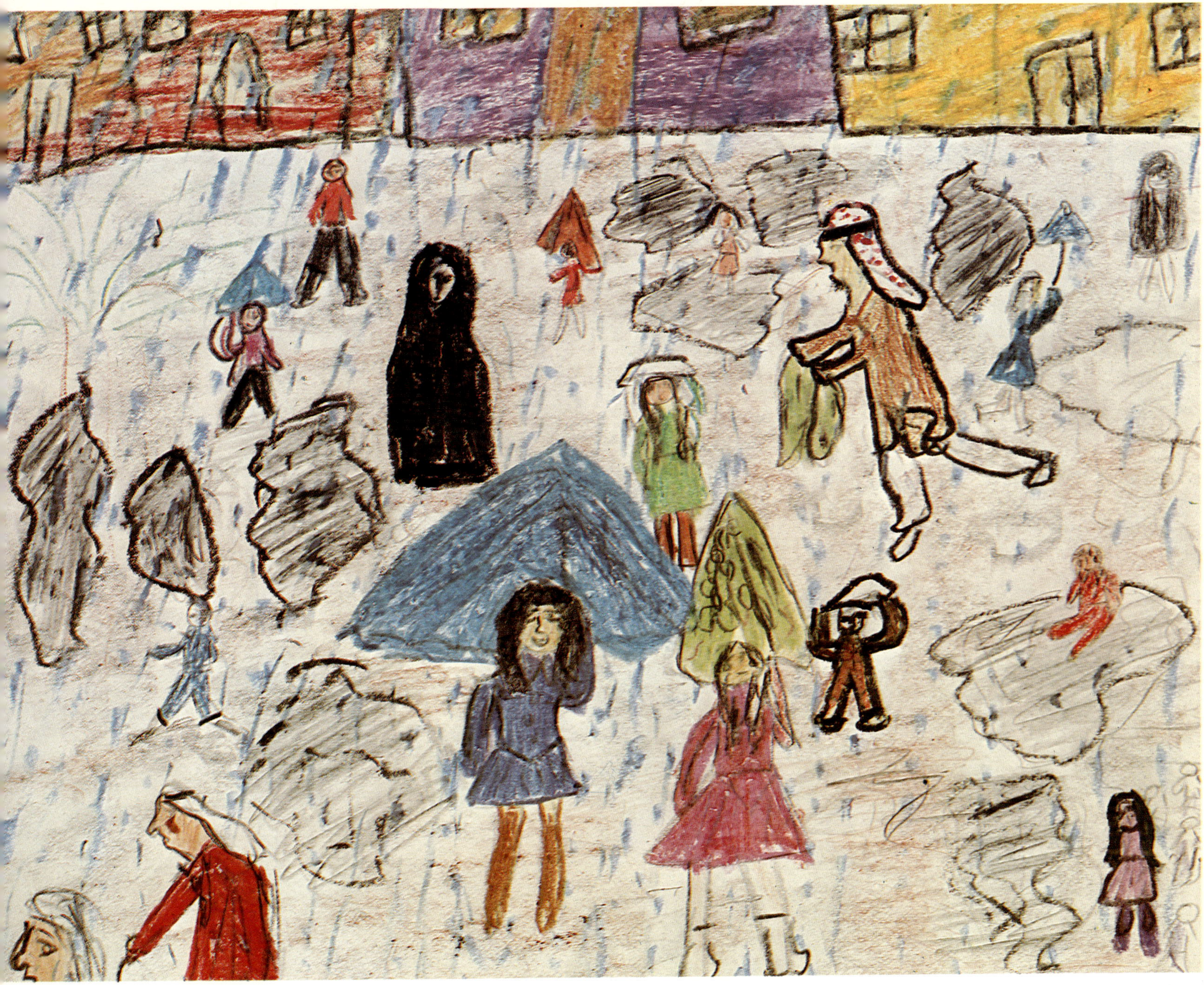

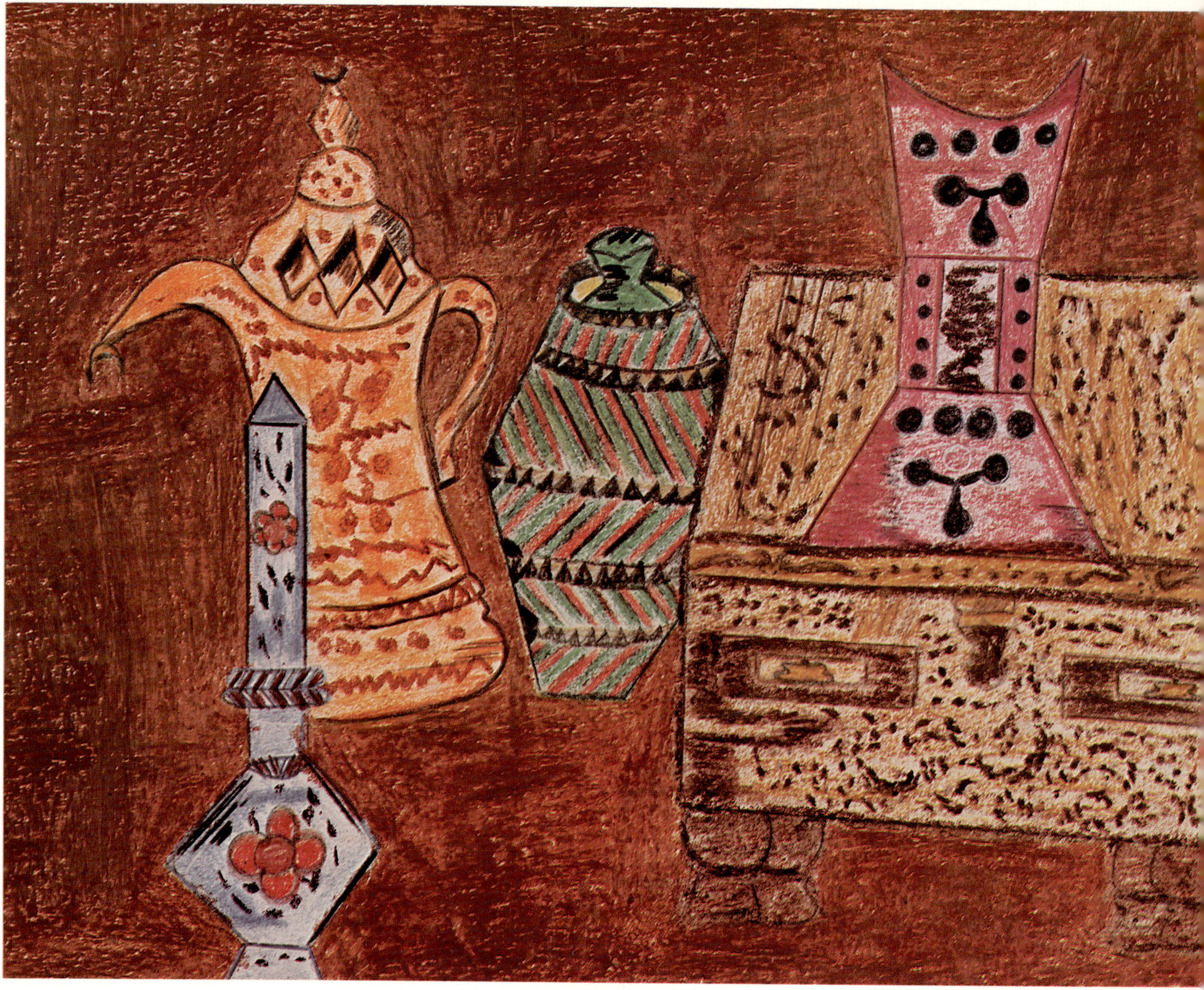

Al Oud: *Incense*

The incense is burned in a brass or silver container studded with mirrors and golden nails. It is called a Mubkhar. The scent that comes from its thick, white smoke is loved by Arabs.

When an Arab entertains visitors in his reception room (majlis), the Mubkhar and the Marash (a flask holding rosewater) are brought in. After guests finish drinking their bitter coffee, men in dishdashas appear. They walk around the majlis pouring rosewater into the extended hands of the guests. Each rubs the rosewater on his hands and face while inhaling the scent of the incense.

It is a well-known fact among Arabs that guests are expected to politely take their leave after the ceremony of the incense and rosewater.

Arabs burn incense as a sign of reverence for their guests.

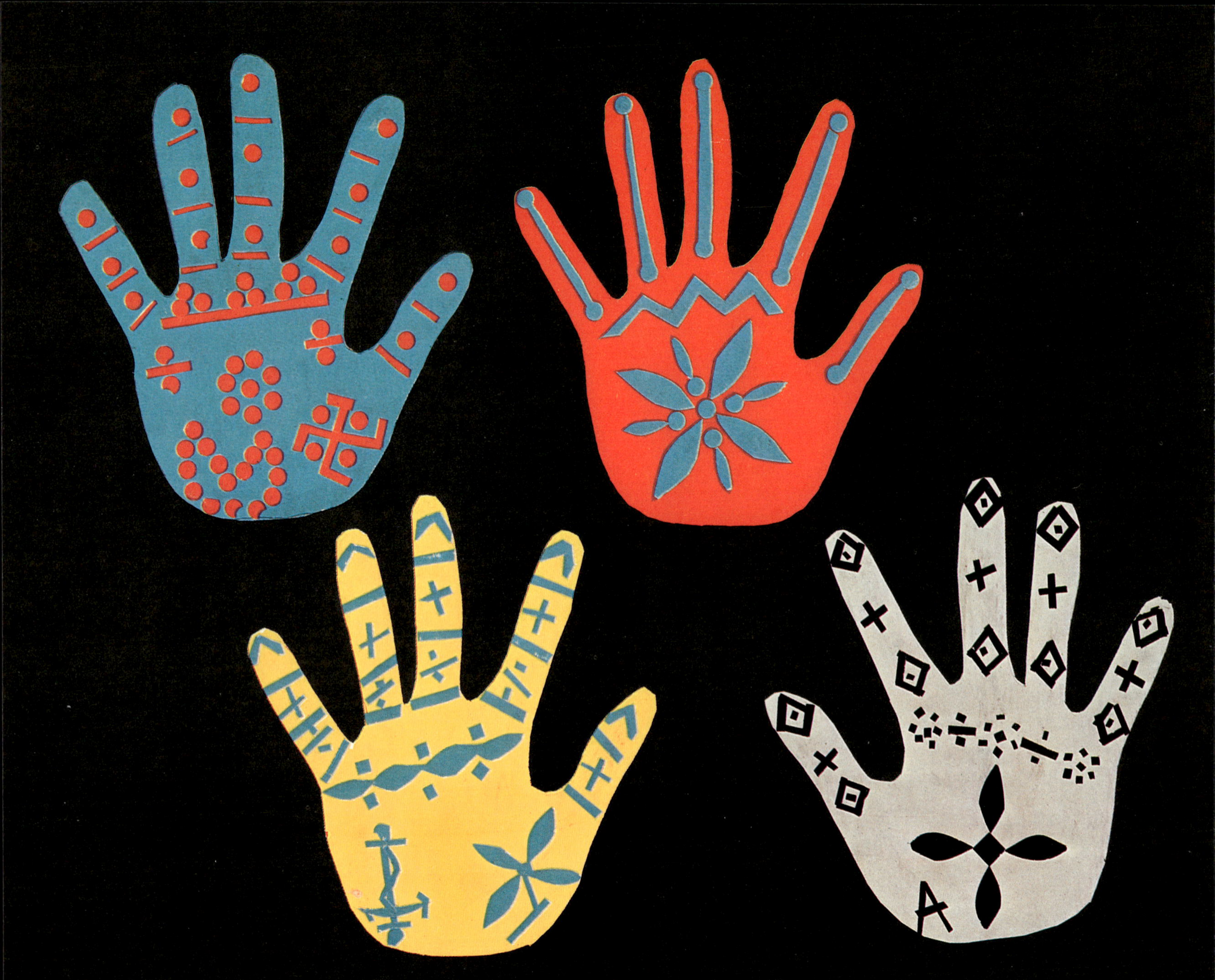

Henna: *Wedding Makeup*

In many Arab homes henna is still used as a form of makeup for the bride on the eve of her wedding.

On Laylat Al Hina, or Henna Night, the bride's relatives and friends gather for a party at her home. They paint intricate henna patterns on her hands and feet. Some sing and dance to entertain the bride.

Arab women use henna not only to make themselves beautiful, but also to protect their skin from too much sun. Sometimes they use it as a medicine to cure headaches, by rubbing it into their hair.

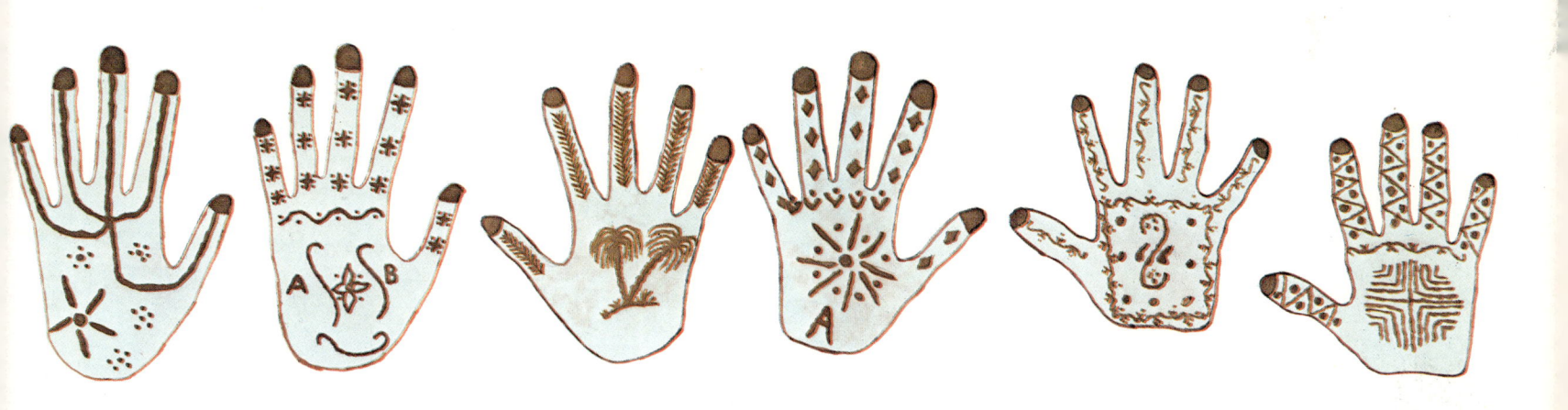

Henna is the powder of a dried bush berry which, if mixed with water in a bowl, turns into a paste of rich red color.

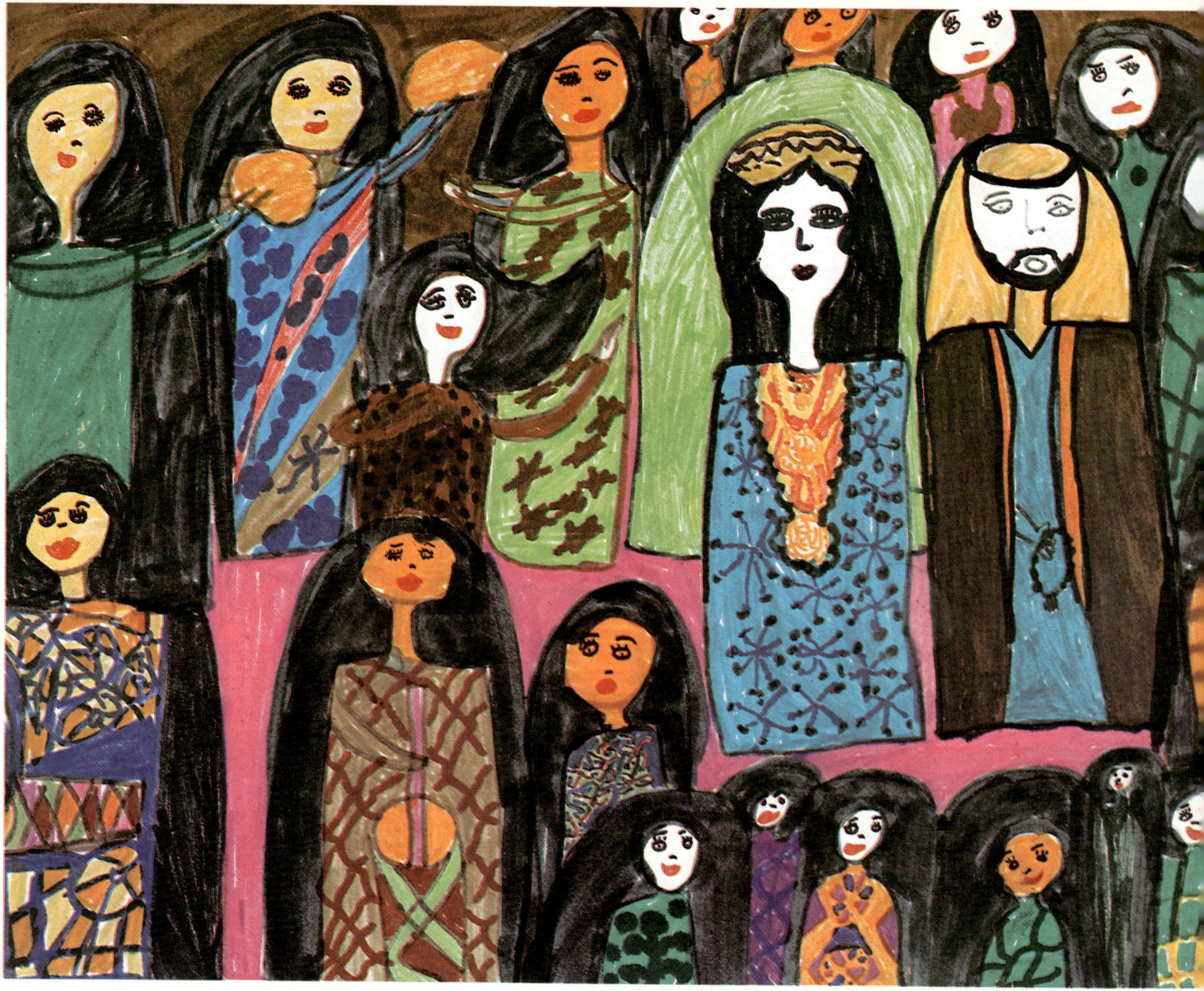

I Zawaj: *The Wedding*

The bridegroom's father visits the bride's father, bringing his son with him. The bride's father welcomes them and listens to their request. He then asks them to come back in a few days for his answer. Meanwhile he asks friends and others in the town about the bridegroom's character and prospects. He also asks his daughter her opinion. If all goes well, the wedding date is set by the two families. Before the wedding takes place a marriage agreement is made in the presence of the Shaikh who inquires about the religion of the young couple. (Shaikh in this case means a representative of the Islamic faith, not the ruler of a tribe.)

A sum of money (a dowry) is given to the girl by her husband-to-be. Westerners often think, wrongly, that when a man pays a dowry he 'buys' a wife. In fact, the dowry is a gift from the man to his future wife. She may spend it as she pleases.

Later on, if a man decides to divorce his wife, he has to give her a larger sum of money. She then returns to her father's household.

The husband is usually responsible for furnishing the home of a newly married couple and taking care of all living expenses.

Whether the marriage which is going to take place is arranged by the parents or the couple themselves, there is a certain procedure to be followed.

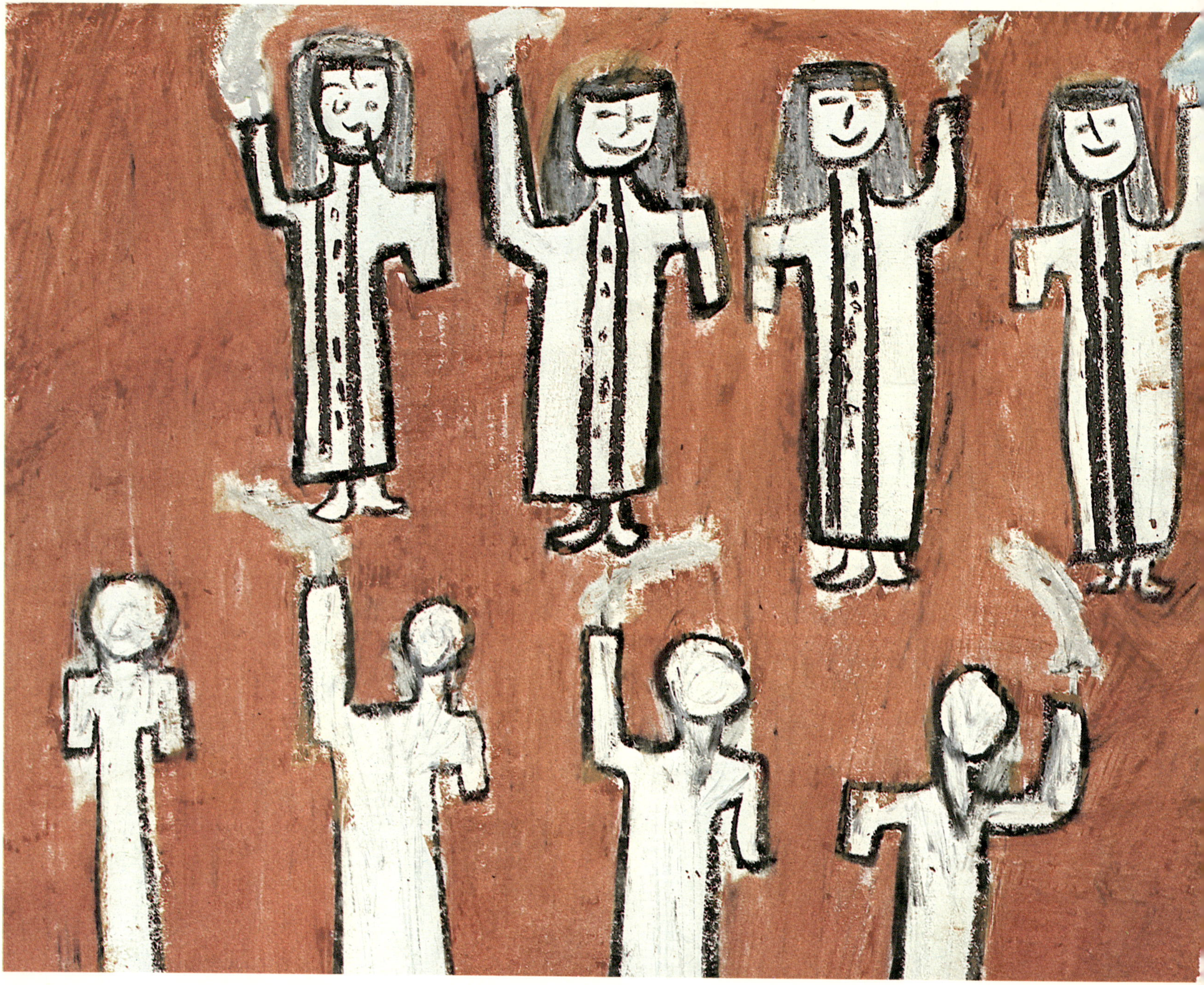

Al Rizeef: *Men's Dance*

They form two long lines facing one another. Then they move forward and back, stamping and singing. Usually each carries a rifle or a thin bamboo cane. The two rows chant songs of praise to the tribe and their ruler, the Shaikh. The men dance to the strong beat of drums and taarah — a tambourine made of animal skins. The Shaikh and distinguished men of the tribe take part in the dance.

Chant:
Too much wishing and talk
Nothing can achieve
Great peoples' glory is in their deeds
And those who seek power and knowledge
Will read the Arabs' history
And do similar deeds

Rizeef is the dance of the desert. Men singers and dancers perform it in war, and in times of peace on happy social occasions such as weddings and during Eids.

Al Muradaa: *Women's Dance*

Two rows of women step backwards and forwards while chanting songs praising the beauty of Arab women.

Chant:
Oh, look at the moon traveling East
In the desert it lays and sleeps
Say hello to those who in the desert sleep
And greet the one whose scent is sweet

On the night before weddings and during Eids women gather in their own part of the house with friends to chant songs and dance.

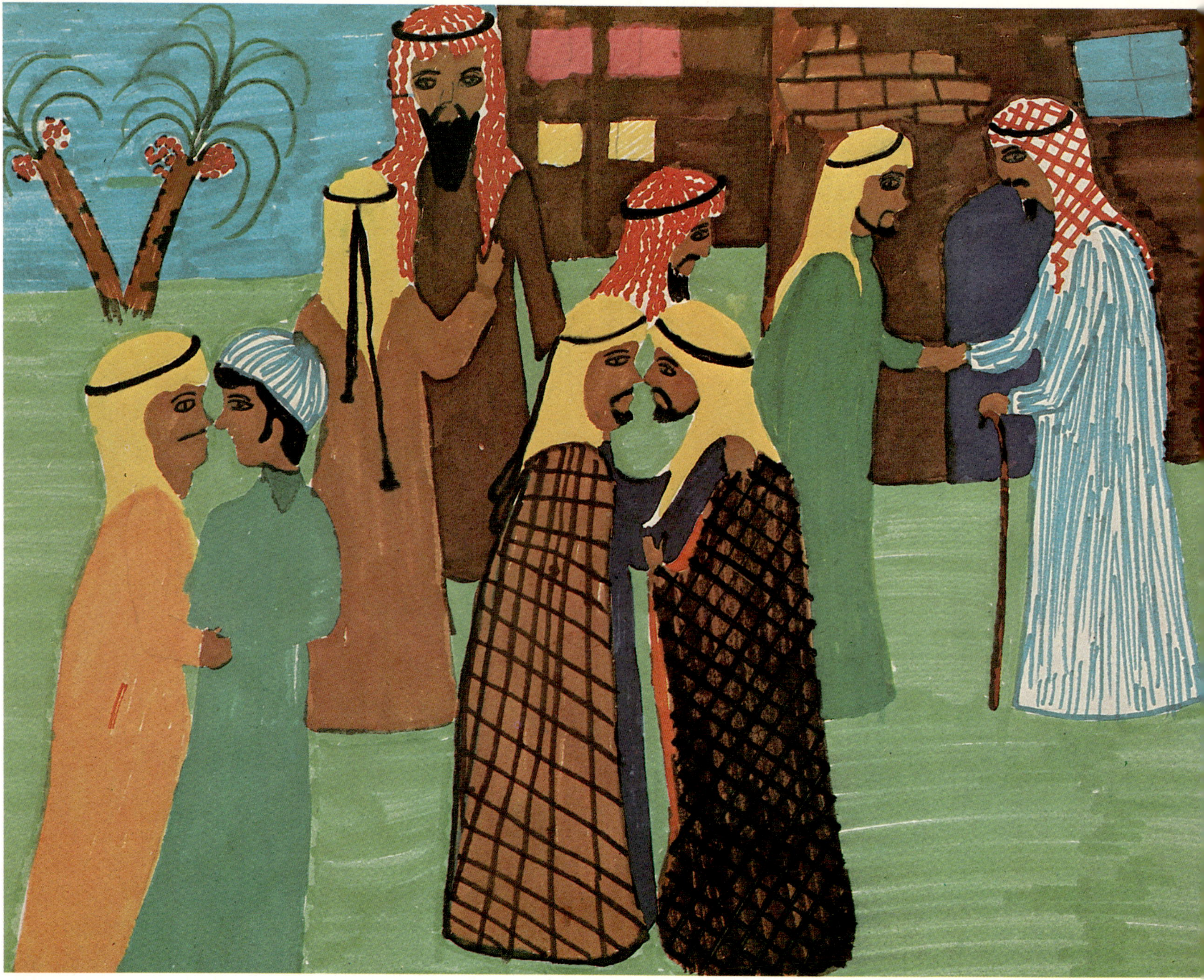

'Eid Mubarak': *'Blessed be your celebration'*

Eid means celebration. The two most important Muslim celebrations are Eid Al Adha and Eid Al Fitr. Eid Al Adha, the Feast of Sacrifice, is celebrated at the end of the Hajj. (Hajj means a pilgrimage. A special time is designated each year when Muslims may make a pilgrimage to Mecca). Eid Al Fitr marks the end of Ramadan, the month of fasting.
At dawn on the first day men gather in mosques for prayers and many of them then visit the cemetry for remembrance of their dead. Then they visit the Shaikh, relatives and friends. The women stay at home.
For children Eid days are full of joy from sunrise to sunset. They dress in their best clothes and go from house to house saying 'Eid Mubarak' to their neighbors who may give them money or sweets (Eidaya).

Eid is a time of good will. People open their hearts, pay their respects to others and exchange compliments and kisses.

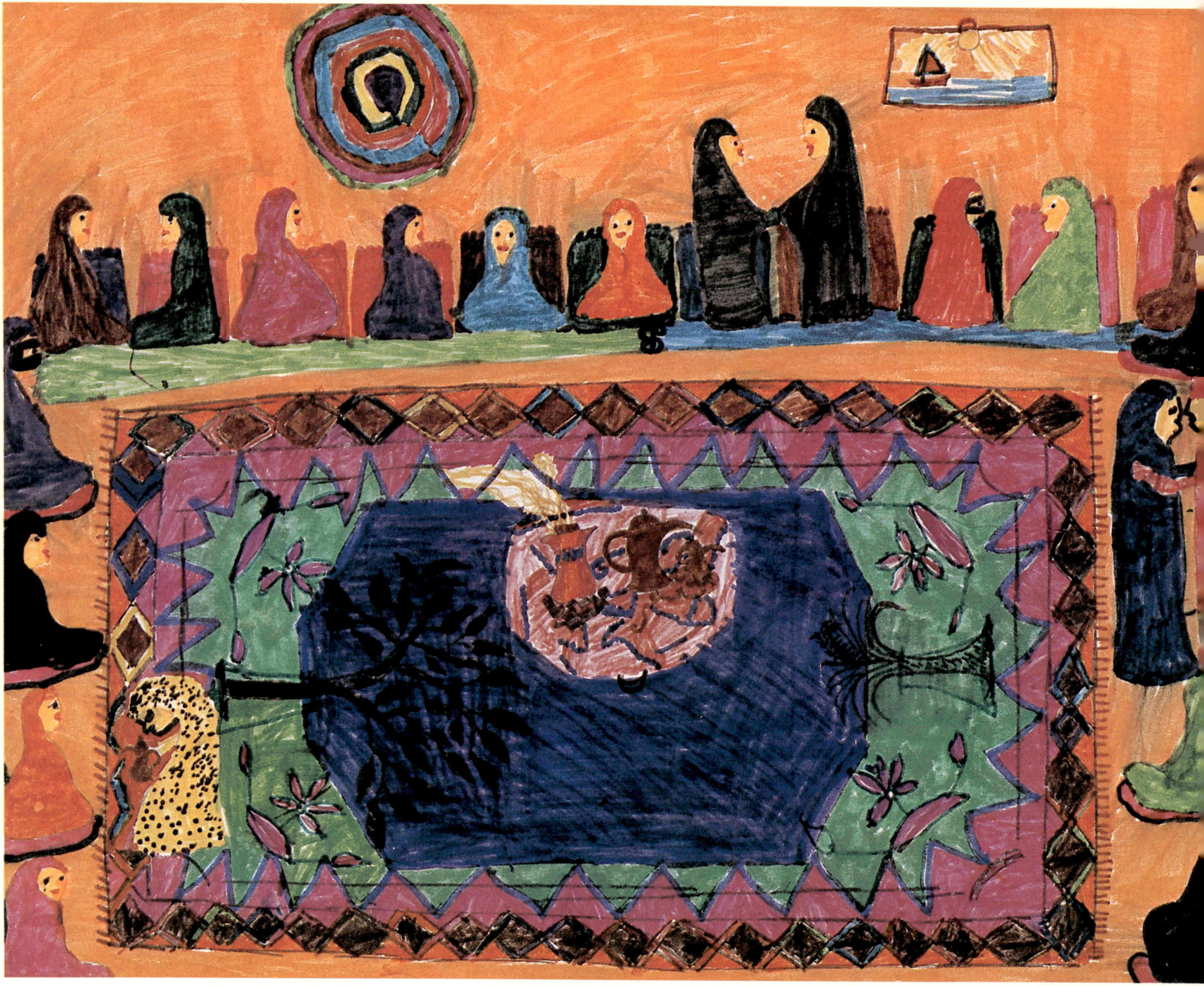

Salaam Al Eid: *Courtesy Calls*

When a woman visitor first enters the sitting room (majlis) of a friend or relative, it is customary for her to kiss her hostess on each cheek, saying 'Eid Mubarak'. After that she greets the others present. The hostess then addresses every lady in turn by her name, asking about her health and that of her family. Meanwhile maids circulate around the room offering soft drinks, sweets and coffee. The coffee cup is refilled each time it is empty until the person drinking it shakes the cup from side to side to signal that no more is wanted. After the coffee is served, two maids enter the sitting room; one holds an incense burner (Mubkhar), the other a flask (Marash). The one carrying the Marash pours rosewater in the extended hands of the ladies who rub it on their faces and in their hair. The second maid holds the Mubkhar while each guest inhales the fragrant incense. At the end of this ceremony it is polite for the ladies to take their leave. The whole visit lasts for about an hour.

On the second day of celebration the women visit the homes of relatives and friends. Some may also pay their respects to the Shaikha, the wife of the Shaikh.

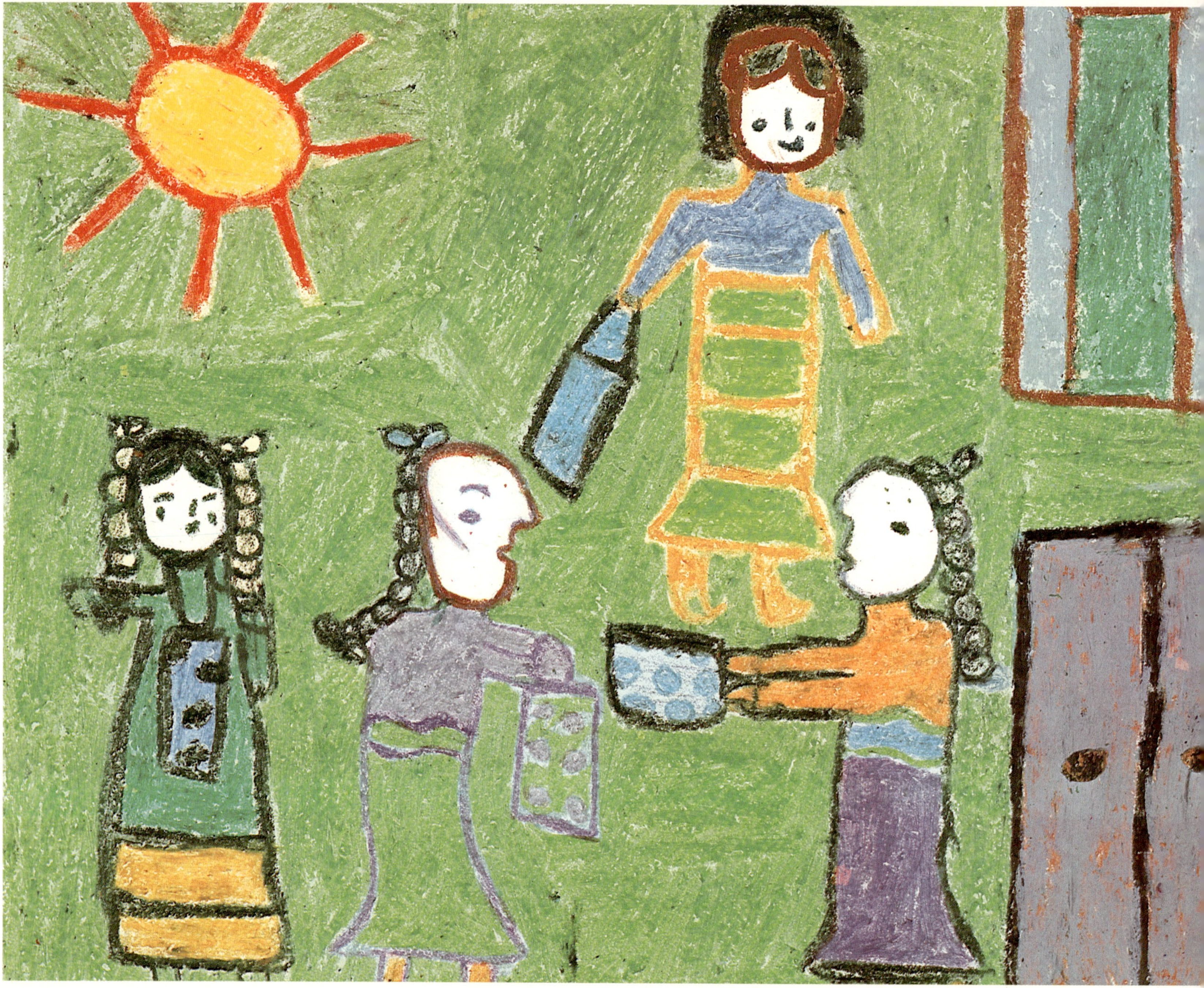

...d Al Adha: *The Celebration of the Sacrifice*

...his practice began in the days of Ibrahim the
...ophet, who had a son. The story is told in the Koran.
...llah wanted to test Ibrahim's obedience to him. He
...ppeared to Ibrahim in a dream and ordered him to kill
...s son, Ismail. The day of sacrifice came. On a hill
...utside Mecca Ibrahim was about to do what Allah
...d ordered. Suddenly he heard His voice commanding
...m to stop. Allah told him to sacrifice a ram grazing
...arby instead. For hundreds of years since that time
...ell-to-do Muslims have been imitating this act of
...crifice. Once a year on Eid Al Adha they kill a sheep
...d give both raw and cooked meat and rice to the
...or.
They do this to thank Allah (God) for his kindness.

...n the first day of Eid Al Adha well-to-do Muslims share their
...od with the hungry and the poor.

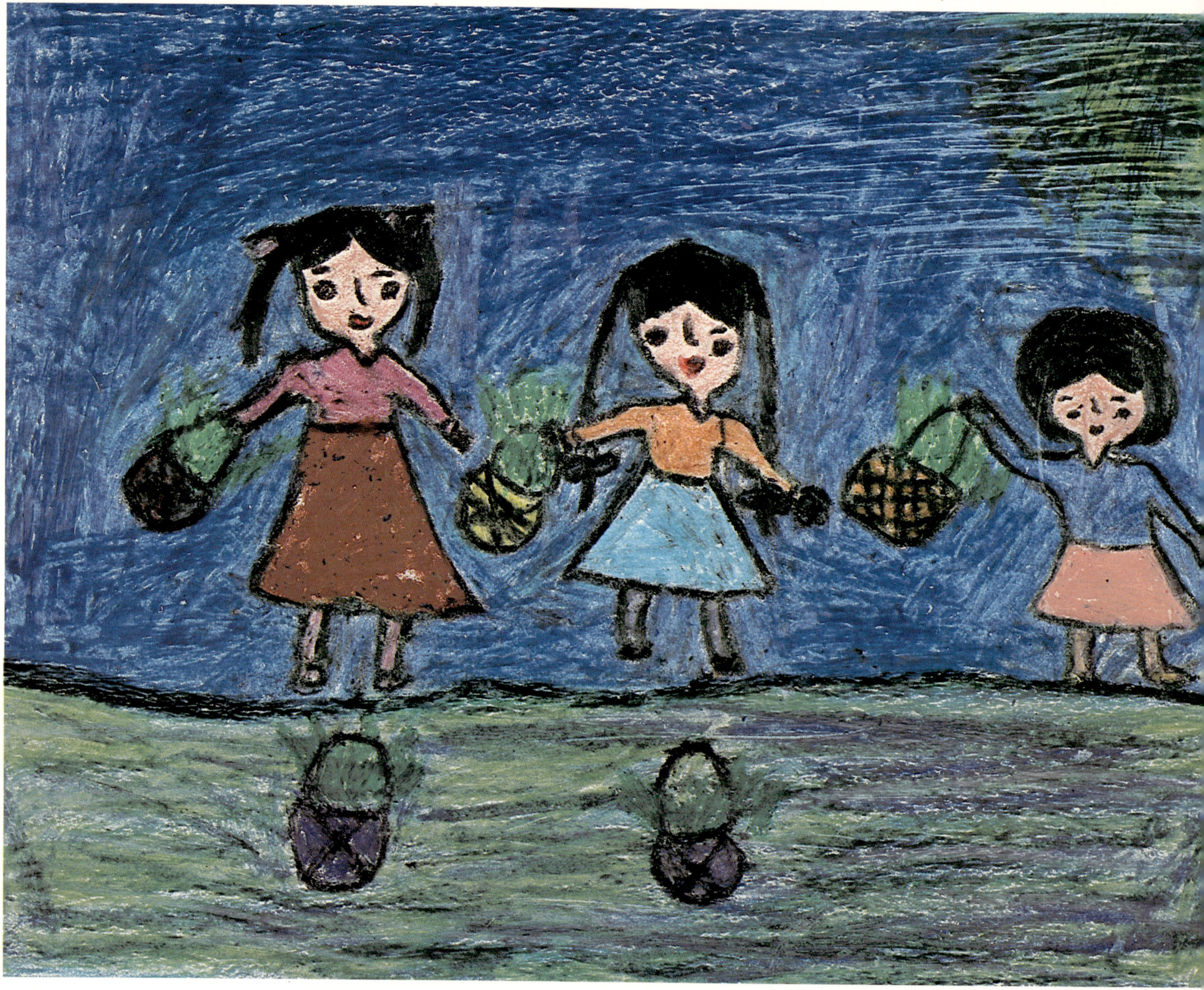

...ya Biya: *Children's Sacrifice*

...eeks before this event children in the Arabian Gulf
...ow a plant called hiya biya. They plant it in a little
...sket with a rope attached on each side. The basket is
...ng on the wall and watered every day.
...On the night of the sacrifice children gather in small
...oups and take their baskets to the seashore. They
...ing them as they walk along singing songs, then toss
...e baskets into the sea.

...y hiya
...ave you food
... Eid Day don't think
... speak badly of me,
...y hiya biya

...ope our Eids will always
...me
...d that our enemies' joys
...k in the seas
...odbye my hiya biya

...ya Biya is a plant sacrificed by children on the eve of Eid Al Adha.

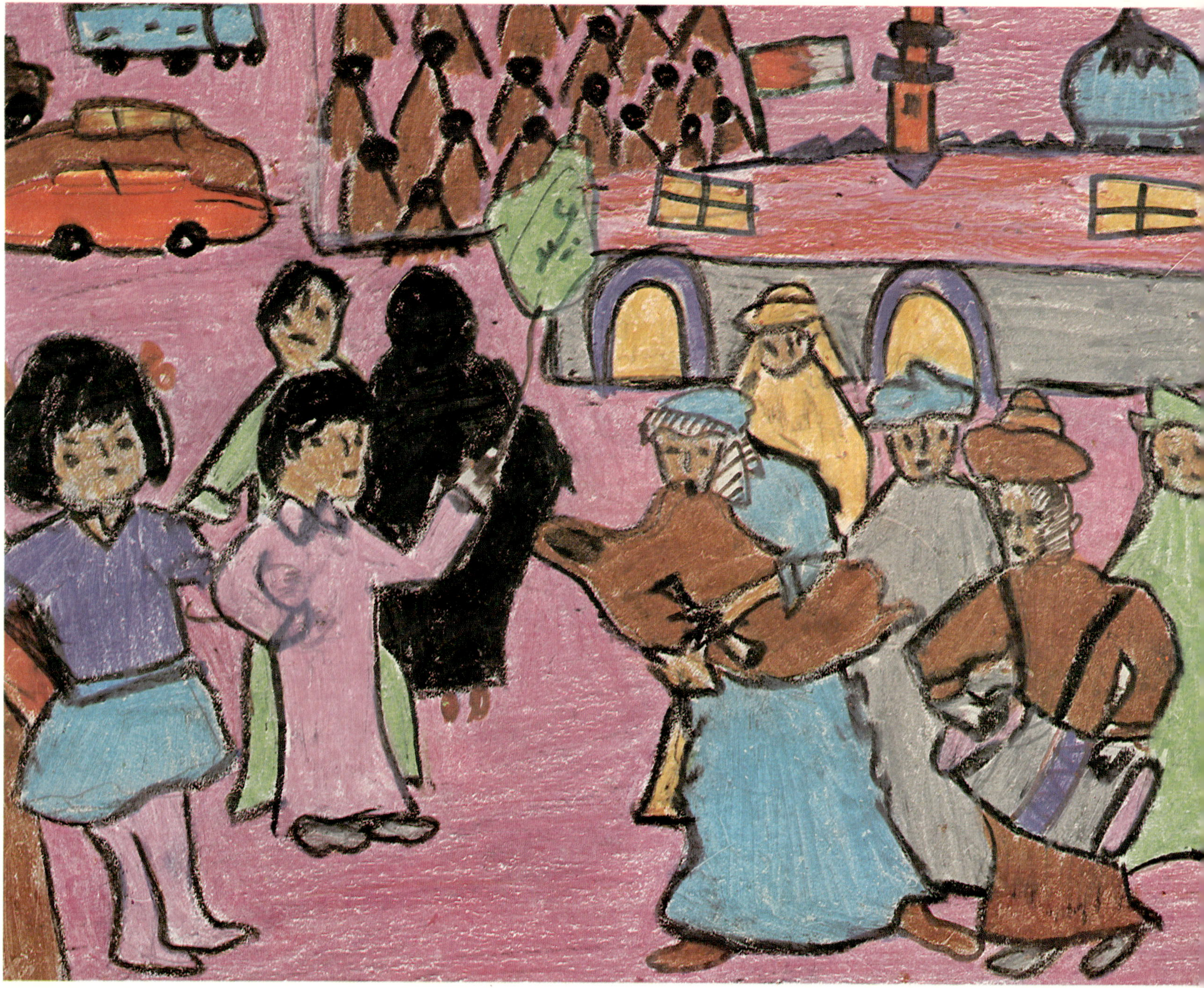

Tubool: *The Band*

[M]usicians play drums, taarah and jerba to accompany [th]e singers. The taarah is a tambourine made of [go]atskin. The jerba can be called Arabian bagpipes. It is [th]e body of an animal inflated with air, with a pipe [att]ached to one leg. When the musician blows through [th]e pipe, it makes a wheezing, whistling sound. [S]ometimes young girls dance between two rows of [si]ngers, shaking their heads to show off their long, [sil]ky black hair.

[O]n every Eid and during wedding celebrations bands of men and [w]omen make music and sing and dance in open grounds where [pe]ople gather to watch.

Furaisa: *The Wooden Horse*

A man wears the wooden head of a horse and covers himself with a colorful cloth tied around a wooden box body. He dances to the music of jerba and drums. The Furaisa goes from house to house during Eids with a group of six to ten men. Some sing, some play musical instruments. Furaisa, the wooden horse, dances in the middle. They perform in the courtyards and afterwards expect a gift of money. Sometimes the young boys of the neighborhood who like to sing join the group and follow it around.

Furaisa is the name of a wooden horse used during celebrations to entertain children.

Girgaoun: *Mid-Ramadan Songs of Praise*

In the month of Ramadan children go from one house to another singing special songs of praise to those who fast. In return they receive handfuls of nuts and sweets which they put in long, narrow cloth bags (kees).